SOLACE

[poems for the broken season]

Chris Wheeler

Copyright © 2019 Chris Wheeler

All rights reserved. This book or any portion thereof may not be reproduced or used in any manner whatsoever without the express written permission of the publisher, except for the use of brief quotations in reviews. For information, please contact the publisher.

ISBN: 978-0-578-60765-8
ISBN: 978-0-578-60767-2

Library of Congress Control Number: 2019918222

Any reference you find to historic events,
real people or places that might take offense:
they're all used fictitiously,
or at least, surreptitiously,
or maybe subconsciously (in my defense).

The author wishes to thank the following publications for their hospitality to selected poems in this collection: Barren Magazine, Foundling House, Fathom Magazine, and Kingdoms in the Wild.

Front cover image and original art by Josie Koznarek.
Book design by Josie Koznarek.

Printed by Ingram Spark, in the United States of America.

First printing edition, 2019.

Chris Wheeler
13980 County Road 12
Middlebury, IN 46540

chriswheelerwrites.com
jkoznarek.com

To Linnea

TABLE OF CONTENTS

introduction / iv
solace / ix

WINTER

chicago in season i / 3
steel / 4
snuffed / 5
vinterfelt / 6
cŵn annwn / 8
the silent fringe of / 8
wendigo / 9
advent / 12
peace / 13
snowbird / 14
first snow / 15
You, once / 17
benediction / 18

SPRING

chicago in season ii / 23
invocation / 24
stay with me / 25
nestling / 26
receive / 27
spring cleaning / 28
elements / 29
a leaf, taken / 32
nadia / 33
triptych for Holy Week / 34
(soon) / 38
majestic / 39
blackbird / 40

SUMMER

chicago in season iii / 45
julep / 46
that postmodern crap. / 47
ode to the city / 48
kyrie for july fourth / 49
starling / 50
placeless / 51
chasing heaven / 52
golf-ball sized hail / 53
three moments of fatherhood / 54
leech / 60
call and response / 61
rainplay / 61
quiet / 62

AUTUMN

chicago in season iv / 67
familiars / 68
through fathoms / 69
blanks / 70
US-20 in october / 71
bleeding in, bleeding out / 72
suspension lament / 73
ode to autumn / 75
but now i see / 76
bon-fire / 77
crowns / 78
perhaps the sea / 79
wanton / 80
and there will come a time / 81
burn on steady / 82

the giving of thanks / 86

INTRODUCTION

Solace, by definition, is relief from pain. It is a soothing influence. In the Old English, that relief is closely tied to the application of truth (as in a soothsayer). As medicine applied soothes the pain of the body, so truth applied soothes the pain of the spirit.

The first truth we encounter is the reality of the pain. It's no mistake that the first sound we make when we enter this world is a cry. We live here, in daily reminders of our frailty, in loss of those we love, in chronic darkness.

These poems, in large part, came out of such seasons of pain, loneliness, despair, darkness, and uncertainty — my own seasons, and those of the people I love. They run along inner lines of tensions between faith and doubt, love and hate, flesh and spirit. Through these poems I've been able to lean into the broken seasons until they crack open, until I can see what's really inside them.

And the marrow of it all is grace.

The darkest seasons of my life have wrought the greatest clarity, the truest truth: that I am desperately in need, and desperately loved. I don't have what it takes. No answer to my brokenness lies within me. True freedom is born out of giving up, realizing that I am as good as dead. And when I come groveling to the door of my Father's house pleading to be made of some use to Him — He rushes out to greet me and welcomes me in love, as a true son. I am not lovable because I am useful. I am lovable because He loves me.

This is the solace I cling to.

Poetry can be many things: a desperate prayer, an epiphany in stillness, a passionate proclamation, or a well-reasoned argument. It can be a humorous aside, a sly remark, or distilled joy. The poems in this collection are all of these things.

But mostly, to me, they are a light in the dark.

My prayer is that they will be so for you as well.

— *Chris Wheeler*

Again we come
to the resurrection
of bloodroot from the dark,

a hand that reaches up
out of the ground,
holding a lamp.

Wendell Berry

solace

I would give birth
to a thousand fluttering
things: paper swans and
metal wings, a sewing
needle and a swelling drop
of red that splashes into blue,
the springing up of asters
on the eve of winter, wells
in each eye and the bucket that
drops into blackness, into the
cold sweet water of this cold
sweet earth.
                For within me
it coils: springs and gears
and divots, graven images,
sandy boards smelling of smoke
and incense, the heady perfume
of bread and wine intermingled. Within
me lie fields on fire, fields thrumming,
fields of fallen clay figures, barren fields
brimming, fields of gold and copper fading
deep into cobalt, fields of wheat, and
the lines fall in pleasant places and
the boundary stones mean little and
the air is solace.

                Yes, I would give birth, if only
to care while she was in my keeping, if only to wrap a
woolen scarf around her neck and lace up
her boots, to see her wander into the wasteland
with nothing but mittens and her tongue
stuck out stubborn to the left,
to know I may never see her again,
and yet to give birth.

WINTER

chicago in season

i.

Dragons of the north
puff smoke and heat from lungs in
cold weather exhale.

—

Someone started a
word search in the heated grids
at my brown line stop.

—

The rooftops are hosts
to blue steam demons writhing
from every pipe.

—

Under Jackson bridge
the river finally breaks
and flows in fractals.

—

It's cold today, says
Chi-town, at fifty below,
but not as cold as…

steel

If only
the fires of autumn
burned on beyond
the snow, melting back
the all-father grey
like the back of the aged wolf
rippling across the sky in pursuit.
I want to savor
the bud-green, mud-brown of spring,
the sun-yellow, splash-blue of summer,
the leaf-red-mulch-purple of autumn —
anything else.

But
all I
smell
is steel.

snuffed

A cliché:
I have been said
and wish to be unsaid.
Coffee, silence, blank page,
the lingering doubt that this
was ever a good idea — a spark!
Snuffed, better in my head. Is it
doubt or have you left me
wordless? I have emptied
myself to be filled, I have feasted
and remain empty.

If I had no words,
if silence crept to my lips
and placed its finger to them,
if darkness filled my hands,
pressed down, shaken together
and running over, if I could
never see again,
would I
still love you?

vinterfelt

I went back to my childhood home
amid the rustle of an old year,
and walked the back acre trails again.

The staccato stems of soybeans
stripped clean by wandering deer
are the only harvest left.
Like long-observed traditions, they appear here
and disappear there, in and out of the drifts.
The wind off the field is honest.
It blows through me with force,
scent-shot with woodsmoke, steel, and snow-soaked sod.
The trail feels odd somehow,
but the wind I know too well.
I touch the naked maple set along the acre's edge
and branded memories come to mind.
I was present here, once.
I was placed.

Is this the way of renewal?
Seeing the old by seeing it new,
the forgotten through the memory?

Absence obscures the roots,
but the damage was done, the mark made,
by things I don't and do recall,
in places I do and don't know now.
The earliest roots run long and deep,
like the smell of a winter field,
like the texture of trees.

So I stand
on the edge of the field
and open my heart to the wind,
to hear again the stories
of the struggles and triumphs
borne in small places
of an old country, flanked by fields,
tied up tight in acre-lines.

We talk of impact,
as if by force, we will be remembered.
as if by speed and escape,
old pains will pass away.
But it is in
slow erosion,
ice seeping into rock,
smelling of shrapnel, cold and hot at once;
the caress of a yellow sky
at four in the afternoon, eastern;
the silent light of Indiana
broken only by sparrow-call;
the wind streaming from the rich and fallow field:

These
are embedded so deep
my skin has closed over them.
These
can't be removed.
These make us, if we let them,
and when we return to them broken by motion,
they embrace us as old friends.

And I left that place again.
I leave it more than I stay these days,
but it's good to have a home
that never leaves.

cŵn annwn

Beyond the rolling garlands,
the late stands of autumn leaves
like mantles crowning the day,
a geyser of grey rolls, heaves

itself to the sky. Someone
is undone somewhere, burning,
but the whole sky is clouded
steel, like the shrouded yearning.

Between us fields of young snow
stretch in rows, a muffled front.
The fire is hard to find when
hounds of Gwyn are on the hunt.

the silent fringe of

The silent fringe of
frost lattice on loud windows,
the glow in the pipe.

wendigo

"full of fiction like the blood moon..."
— Penny and Sparrow, "Wendigo"

it is december, and along the path
the spindly fingers of the aspens
clutch at the skull of the moon
above the pale breast of snow.
the path is silent but for the crunch
of bones beneath my boots, and my
breath knows me too well.

well above, the lodge looms, ancient
ancestral home, and when i heard
he had disappeared i said, "who?"
but thirty acres of trackless north
made me hungry. it may sell, but
for now i am the sole occupant.
the woodshed is down the hill.

hills of aspens have long been bereft,
yet they rattle as I approach, angular
skeletons scraping limbs together,
cowering over a deepening tunnel.
my ancestor must have cleared it,
preferring a brisk walk to the ease
of a woodpile stacked close.

close through the maw of the lunging
beast, i am ringed round by a crown
of teeth. at the throat a branch snaps,
but I did not snap it. my eyes sharpen,
the emaciated limbs embrace me and
falsify the haunting, the horror of things
unseen, unknown, and the door ahead.

ahead, the door, and i step briskly,
dread moaning at my heels, bracken
twisting at my toes, and grasp close to
my chest a bundle of cordwood, loosing
one to wield with my right. i peer at the
moonlit stairway to the warm-lit lodge.
it is vacant but for my bootprints.

bootprints beating their way back, in
my periphery a mercurial skeleton
keeping pace beyond the aspens, a
slurry of limbs and my ears detect
a low moaning on the rise, from
the clattering gullet of the thing.
it croons at the tang in the air.

the air beats at my back, grappling
with cuspate claws for purchase, and
the keening appetite behind me sprints
on all fours. i turn my head once, for
an instant, and our eyes meet, and i
taste forbidden flesh, detect my death.
a violent hunger wakes within.

within the entry I stumble, and swing
the branch back in blind defiance. did i
connect? i lose the key. i find the key.
the scraping on the steps is ravenous
and as i cross the threshold a gaunt fang
slips through my boot. i kick the door closed
and lie listening. something keens.

keen as a blade, the cut is long and clean.
i dress it up and stoke the fire, a battering at
the walls swelling my soul like starvation,
thrumming in my blood. through the frost-rim
i see spindly shadows stalking, but the heat from
my wound rises on the arc of the moon, the night
awakening a hunger.

advent

The deepest days ahead
are hung with tinsel,
wrapped with bows.
The darkness is encroaching
in the hour, seeping slow.
It holds the sun at bay,
waiting like a million eyes,
watching pregnant-bellied skies
for newborn snow.

I am watching sparrows
pruning berries,
shedding clothes.
I wonder as I watch them
just how deep this tunnel goes.
It sinks under the way.
The hollow is the night –
in despair we'll see the light
of newborn snow.

I am fading like a leaf
of fall at frost
whose lifeblood slows.
I am waiting to be
hung and dried and
fragrant like the rose.
I am silent. I will stay
until the hope becomes the hold,
the song of whores and saints of old,
of newborn snow.

peace

      Why
in the season of singing
is my head only lifted
by longing? are my eyes
only brightened by flickers?
do I wince at the light?

      Why
do you take my wrists
and stretch me beyond
the limits, a flayed skin taut
upon the rack, exposed
in the tension? I hear it,
before the drop, as vinegar
to the tongue of the thief,
like the last song of the sparrow.
I linger, stretched to stillness
between your grip
and the chains, and I watch
it flutter away.

      Why
in the season of singing
is my only peace gifted
by sorrow?

snowbird

If not for
seed flung aside
by raucous jays,
the winter
would be lean.

If not for
vibrant plumage
that draws the gaze,
the talons
would be keen.

Let me be
small and brown
and content
with thistledown.

advent

We went to service against the wet, white wind,
our cheeks blushing at its advances.

My daughter asked if there would be snow,
and my son repeated the sound. Mommy said maybe.
In the warm wood sanctuary they lit flames of hope
atop the heads of purple pillars, eternal flames.
Merry signs of threaded gold snaked down the minister's stoll
uncoiling on fields of white.

And You talked
and we sang
of silence,
the moments distilling
drop
by
drop
upon the other,
upon our thirsty tongues.

For a time, we forgot
the weariness and worry,
or maybe
we gained strength
to face it.

Word and Sacrament,
a duo of grace.

We gather again in the narthex,
treats for the old and treats for the young —
my son's favorite part of any church.
He bears a crumpled cookie in each hand
and wonders as he wanders.
I sip church coffee for the warmth.

Then outside we suddenly see
white.
A present magic grows in every tiny chest
and many an old heart. Children all, we crowd at windows,
fogging them with warm cookie breath and exclaiming:
"Snow!"

When we left,
coat-bundled to keep in the heat,
my son suddenly understood this stuff
and raised chubby fingers skyward in awe
to catch the moment.

I thought to myself
that the prayers we need answered most aren't even the
ones we utter,
and the blessed manna fell in clusters to the blacktop lot,
and it was
an answer.

You, once

I would live as if You had
brushed my lips with Your finger
not a second ago,
lifted a lock of hair back,
and looked me in the eyes.

I would live as if nothing
mattered but that moment,
that my days would be spent
in recall
and repetition.

My days are not spent
this way, so
I wish them gone
for the sake of tomorrow,
for maybe tomorrow
I will be better,
tomorrow I will be closer,
tomorrow
I will be...

Tomorrow
I will kiss You,

but until
tomorrow,
kiss me.

benediction

I am leaving.
Coat-muffled, booted,
scarved, gloved,
broiling in my own body heat.
I long for sub-zero in the moment,
willing to enter the eternal
white-caped horizon beyond the door,
even as I hate to leave the warmth
of you.

Grant me
the solace of one more
Word — even in farewell,
that it may echo in my ears
on the long walk home.

Grant me
the comfort of one more
embrace — our roots entwined
and holding to our chests
that which matters most.

Grant me
the warmth of one more
kiss — brand my cheek
in memoriam, in naming
of the love we knew here,

and thus anointed
I will go forth in wilder worship.

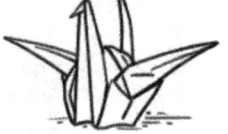

chicago in season

ii.

Small bundles of joy,
folded heads and hands unsheathe
the warm afternoon.

—

Warm sheets and showers
embrace me of a morning:
rainy Chicago.

—

His netted cap says
"Trainman;" he props it back and
drinks smoke to pass time.

—

Tracks of a robin
wax eternal, outlasting
set and sealed concrete.

—

Something green always
blooms between the cracks, even
if it's only weeds.

invocation

Isn't there inherent hope
in dawning, of things doing,
as there is in dusk, of death?
We are children of the promise
long before we penetrate it.
We must live to the last
before we begin...

stay with me

Snap me something jagged,
Snap me open like a shell
of something precious, stabbing gold
into people's eyes like the glory I cannot know.
For I am jagged and blind to my own,
I am shrapnel in my brain.
I am earth-shaking,
a second lasting an eternity,
but I am blind
until I look.

There are many miracles, like earthworms in the dirt
or the pillbug on its back that makes my children smile,
or the centipede that scurries like the danger.
We are all of these and none at once,
giants in a world of giants,
and I wish that I could stay to see them through.

Stay with me, my miracle,
my solitary jewel, set in silver like the moon,
my butterfly blooming from the end of its capsule,
squirming life into limpid wings,
my shards of sight when all I can see is golden
my danger in the crevice,
my earth-shaking everything.

All will be new,
all will live again one day,
but until then we are miracles,
fragile as the mechanism in the chrysalis,
delicately telling time
until the day.

nestling

I woke today
to scrabbling in the nest,
an irresistible urge
to leap.
In looking past the edge
of all I knew
I saw a vast expanse,
alive and impossible,
and in taking a lungful of it
I knew that
embracing air
was all it would take.

So I woke to the world,
I woke to the sky,
and I took it as it stood:
empty and full.
In climbing to its back
I spread my wings
and met the ground
violently,
like an old friend.

And I knew I could
never walk again.

receive

It's taken years of You
reversing my fears, of me
inhaling the tears of a cursed world unhinged,
lunging in my lungs for every gasping breath.

It isn't enough to believe in grace once and move on, an
honorary member.
I need to receive grace twice, thrice, and forever
until I know my need so thoroughly
that only the gifted whole heaven will do,
and I wait, uplifted soul, to You.

We do not live and move and have our being by the courage of our hearts,
but by the coronary explosion of His,
Who gives and loves and grants us seeing eyes and willing hearts to detonate,
willing lives to watch and wait.

And so each day
reminds us that life itself is grace.
And so each day
is treasured, measured at heaven's pace.
And so each day
is where I find that I am to be found,
and tethered fast to You,
weathered and broken and blue.

I am a bird perched in persistent song,
who thirsts for the sky,
empty and full and true.

spring cleaning

I'm ready for spring cleaning, trees,
you bristling, eager brooms —
to sweep away dust bunny clouds and marvel at swept rooms.
I want to take and scrape you
'cross this spot behind the lines.
When you scrub it right it's crystal,
and it positively shines.

I'm ready for spring cleaning, rain,
you capsuled jars of clean —
to spritz you over old brown fields and turn your edges green.
I want to wash away the mud
from heirlooms in the sink.
All we need is one warm bath
to come out wrinkly pink.

I'm ready for spring cleaning, wind,
you Hoover of the earth —
to shake us loose and send us out with noise and frantic mirth.
Tell me Someone is awake
and cleaning while I sleep,
that when I wake the world
will have woken in its keep.

elements

i. the taste of earth

My children eat sand,
a curiosity turned
granular, just like I did
when I was their age,
and that is why, my child,
I hope you've learned
your lesson, don't go
around eating what we're
made of, it's not
palatable.

ii. the smell of smoke

like he's burning garbage
behind the house, a familiar
flavor once, acrid next,
like maybe he's burning your
box of baseball cards or just
some newspaper, or both of
them together.

from the cherry at the end of
the cigar that I got at your
wedding. I lit it last night.
It tasted okay but I don't know
cigars. I just felt fancy
and sad and didn't
inhale any.

as I drive by, pinching like
it did when we buried you
that day. It got in everybody's
eyes, and your baby sobbed
for other reasons: signals by
the gravesite of the things
I don't talk about. Why is
everything burning?

iii. the sound of air

Warm cinnamon
between us, clinging
to your lips, parting
at the flex of air, the
internal vibrations,
lung to lung, mouth
to mouth, and eye to
eye. It lingers for that
moment, the air between,
and in the hesitation,
Icarus at the apex,
the moment after
"I love you" and before —

If I heard it would it
change the way you
held me?

iv. the impact of water

I feel rain coming.
The light dims but it's something above me
casting shadows. I am immersed in clouds,
fracturing into mist and drizzle, a collapse.
I am writing in my journal about
I am posting a picture of
I am arranging my schedule around
I am living my life because

I feel rain coming.
Steady the ominous
death of sun and
warmth for the sake of —

but I wasn't ready.

The wind blows it in, and like it I am wild
with terror at the thought — a thought that
alone I am nothing that
with others I am nothing that
I will always be nothing that
the rain will come to nothing as
the ground is filled with nothing.

Nothing stirs before the storm,
within the eye, except a
solitary
bird
song,
distant,
choked out before the petr-
ichor, I am inhaling other people's
dust and smoke and breath
the things that only I
know of them, the downpour

and I am not good enough alone,
I never will be,
but the rain falls on your headstone
and the same rain falls on me.

a leaf, taken

it's liminal —
gathered family jewels
the sigh of relief
an unfinished blink
liquid embraces long withheld
pulling away + proximity
forms and figures tallying value
viewing by seeing or without
celebration decked in flowers, trimmed photos
taking the leaf to its zenith
an anointing of rain

    running
        down the beards of gardeners
        preparing planting beds
    running
        over upturned cups
        of umbrellas,
    running
        sweet across my cheek,

lifting us into a wilder earth
nails tapping to the wood and
the dampening dust on the lid
    under the lids
    all around the latch,
glancing, the beams with the particle
meteors plummeting

cooling density and the long sleep,
the long and faithful rest,
a new thing for each and
older than every other —
solitary, an epiphany;
en masse, an exultation of eyes.

nadia

dark and sweet
perpetually suspicious
she squalls, a tiny finger
wrapped around

mine:
a suture to my scar
a judgment on the world
an acceptance of it
curiosity
hunger

the sound of life
is protest.

triptych for Holy Week

i. absentia

I wake to the wrong
in this unfamiliar,
for never have I known a day without breath,
or a moment bereft of Divinity.
Here it is
a string of empty sentences,
a filmy negative:
absence.

It sticks to me,
seeping in through cell walls.
Pitch and tar: a network of scars
dissolving under translucent skin,
as if blood was black
and black was blood.
Midnight is needling in my veins,
and for a moment there is
the violent silence between spark and ignition,
and blood bursts into consuming flame.
I, too, consume
the void.

ii. limbo

Waiting was never easy.
The frequent settling frosts coat my fields in cobwebs.
My ancient static stations have (of old) been places picked clean,
and the cross encircles my dead, suspended by a thread invisible.
What place do dreams have here?

To me it is less about
isolation or overpopulation
and more about the amount of me present.
To me it is less about
blinding light or stifling dark,
and more about who is blocking both.

I notice the dive
more by motion than intention, as it stutters on my cheek,
and blinks an eyelash in my temple.
How close You are, and how far:
What place does hope have here?

To me You are more about
incense and entrance through thicker smoke,
than You are about breathing easy.
To me You are more about
affection and caress and the touch of lips to life and limb
than You are about washing hands.

In limbo, loss has a name.
What place does
love have here?

iii. absolutio

Once I dreamed
of a blackness silent but once, to speak:
"Release"
and all else fell still.
In the after-echo was a gathering storm
of pinpricks,
as if the veil overhead was pierced by
a million falling angels,
and filtering through the ensuing sieve
came a beckoning increase.
It was the edge of glory,
the very margin of a sweeping light.

Then the microscopic became fearsome
and tore the world from its hinges,
shaking it in joyous, canine frenzy.
We were fetched, and brought forward,
and thrown far afield to return,
to forever fall forward.

And the light blinded us so that we might see,
through saliva and soil, the ceiling we knew
split from side to side as a ribcage parted,
to reveal
the figure of Utter Fullness
ascending,
a Lamp to light the way,
and to gather all lamps in radiance.
In the train of rising trumpet blast,
there was a thrum of budding thunder
as infinity bloomed in time.

I paused,
remembering my hell.
My Lover slipped His arm beneath me,
and embraced me with His right.
He stripped me of my chrysalis,
and I took flight.

(soon)

(in memory of the 2019 Sri Lanka Easter bombings)

The sun goes down
each night, a daily death
wrapped in the night and
multiplied, like my vapor days, anew.

Today was Easter,
and today the sun will also set.

And I, old and new,
cradled in midnight,
nestled in Dawn —
I will remember Easter,
and tomorrow
I will remember Easter again.
For, saints, we will wake
                        (soon)
to a newer morning,
awash with Glory, and weeping

Tomorrow
the terror of the night
may still perch on my shoulders,
may still dwell in the darkness, a living, breathing mass.
The life blood of Your children
may still flow from their veins,
may still stain the walls of Your house, the price of worship.
We are
       now,
       not yet,
       will be.   I have no words for the
                         night of this day
                         but one:
                                      (soon)

majestic

"Then you shall see and be radiant..." - Isaiah 60:5

I will make you majestic, my child.
I will fill you with rivers 'til you brim
with the wild weight of water,
the freedom of the flood
running in your veins.

I will make you luminous.
I will crown you with the morning,
like the sun across the ramparts
at the dawn of everything, a trumpet
call of light, a blast of fire in the night.

I will set my rod in your hand,
a staff of parting on the rise,
pleasant paths through walls of water.
Wander far afield
as you will, my child,
far afield
yet nearer still,
for I AM Home.

Yes, even so, I will make you
a dwelling place:
your walls will be salvation,
your gates will illuminate,
your towers will proclaim
peace, peace to all
in whom I rest,
in you, my child, for
I will make you
Majestic.

blackbird

It's always spring
when I hear it — feathers in the wind,
the hollow-boned chirrup
of the red-winged blackbirds.

They perch
perpendicular
upon the weathered posts,
old boundary spikes
at the edge of the next field,
naked of wire and lonely
as a wintered heart.
They perch there,
like petals pinned to bracken,
a thicket of red —
and they sing.

I don't remember the song
until I hear it, but I think
the lonely thorns
can't help but
love the rose.
And I, a passing soul,
remember things I'd forgotten
and go forth
rejoicing
with the blackbirds.

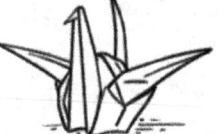

SUMMER

chicago in season

iii.

Silhouette against
peach-tone palette, the tower
is a thick black pen.

—

The drawbridge rising,
his neck extended, slowly:
a brachiosaur.

—

The barge sleeps, nestled
under LaSalle Street bridge with
its sign up: NO WAKE.

—

Rinse and then repeat:
the dangling sudsy spiders
rinse and then repeat.

—

The new station gleams
like new things gleam, and I want
Quincy with her grit.

julep

Sweat on the glass
and sun on the grass —
green in every direction, taking different shades
like we might, if we let it go
and took a single day

to wonder why
You chose these
depths of green
to fill the eye

on this, of all the many, many days.

It's all just brimming now:
ice like expectation
finding healing in the heat,
the slow and steady space
of the spirit and the mint
infusing into tea
like my drink,

while the wind weaves well-being
through a million shifting leaves.

that postmodern crap.

They say we should starve ourselves for faith... or rather they wonder why we don't, because they're doing it. It's all a grain of sand on the tongue and it irritates these oysters when it sticks in their throat. There's a story about it somewhere in There (that Place We Don't Understand) about a pearl and a wedding. I don't remember the reference, I just know it. Do you? It wasn't a rule, just a reality: the kingdom of heaven built on tiny things like eating too much and wasting stuff. He isn't wearing any clothes anymore but that's because they divided them up by lot. We keep doing that. Non-sense is a good word for it, yes, thanks for that. I'll keep using it. If you name it, it's yours. Right? It seems to be a better definition than systematic, fundamental, evangelical. Faith is not seen, just misunderstood, a viable inviolable, I don't but I do, I believe but help my unbelief. I see Him do it so I eat with sinners. I hear Him say it so I say it too. He named me, so I am His. Somehow I believe all this, and I don't even understand why or how it happened. Defining the Definition of all things is foolish. Failures are avenues for the perfection of grace. Go ahead now, line it up. Maybe a pearl or two will come of it... but maybe not.

ode to the city

We are long in the tooth, a lean blood pack on brawny
shoulders thrusting through. The light behind her
images a homing silhouette and she flutters: fierce
beacons of blacktop and steel take shape, and drivers
awake behind the wheel yawn wide. Freedom drifts off;
the long snake slithers slow to it. I was slow to notice it:

the arteries spurting life into streets from all sides, smearing
red over presidents like a parade. The winter has been long
but the blood was thick, always thick, pumping by the gallon
and flowing back by mains, sloshing like a lush through
each intoxication. The muscle is ours: put your ear to the ground,
and you will hear her live again. She's biblical some days.

Don't get too close, she won't let you go. She'll tear you
to pieces and you'll love her for it. When the flow begins
you will see it, you will be it — the pulsing heat and the color.
Would we know her at all if we didn't rouse her on the hour?
Does the heart pump blood or does blood pump the heart?
Don't speak, don't stare, my comrade: remember, take, and eat.

kyrie for july fourth

All the way home I couldn't distinguish
the heat lightning from the fireworks.
They lit up the dark like destruction —
celebration, as ever, wed
with concussions and violent light —
and clouds intercepted static like some luminous football.

Here we are, beating swords into plowshares,
bursting bombs for children to enjoy.
The blast is now made beautiful,
like lightning before the deluge.

And then the fireflies rose glittering on the star-field,
as they always do.
They need no scheduled festival
to adorn the night;
just a single love-lorn insect sparks a horde.

And I thanked God
with guilt in a heavy heart,
for the wars long past and the wars still waged,
those that bought freedom
and those that sold it to the highest bidder.
Some things are worth fighting for,
even to the death.
The difficulty is knowing which ones.

And with all these fires
joining together above us,
I knew again that I knew little,
and in the midst of "Lord have mercy,"
I gave thanks.

starling

The morning after,
feathers of a starling
littered the front lawn.

The cat snoozes sunward,
slit-eyed, in regal repose.

placeless

Would you take me to the fixed place?
I want to be where I can see planets
passing across the sky from a static point,
arcs of light drawing border lines far away
in time lapse, where I can stand still
as the earth moves around me.

Would you take me to the thin place?
I want to be where the air is a familiar color
and the wind smells like the nape of her neck,
the great There in the far off Then. I know so much
and I know so little, but I know my place
exists somewhere, for I miss it.

Would you take me home? To that place
that knows my tongue and tastes like
honey under it, that weighs down the corners
of the world like cisterns, cool and clear and earth
and memory. I could grow
where roots populate, but here I am with feet.

The waiting makes me wonder if my place is no-
where. If so, could you at least take me there?

chasing heaven

It clicks:
the white-washed picket fences
assembling in kind,
along the tick-tock of the
time table. I had
colored in the lines until

it fit:
the perfect shape, the
perfect place,
by all the pretty perfect
faces lined
up silent just in case they saw

it slip:
the sliding smile,
the frown
that quips, the gown
that flickers at
the edge of the eclipse before

it's kissed:
and yet I trembled as I fled,
my heart perched
warm within the pocket
of my coat
as like the dead. And then

it dripped
as liquid from the eye,
and clear, in
running wounds across the sky,
in places I
hold dear: I'm always chasing
heaven like

it's here.

golf-ball sized hail

We were standing in the line
for ice cream when the hail started,
so we hunched our shoulders
and endured
for the sake of
"two scoops peanut butter cup in a waffle cone, thanks."

and it's true,
we were made to eat and drink,
but if I see brimstone
I'm out of here.

three moments of fatherhood

i. her head in the palm of my hand

Down on the eggshell
skull, her head in the palm of my hand, my fingers
split around her perfect ears

                      an eclipse
slides across the ceiling as
she ages, forming adorable tiny
lip-shapes. She vibrates imperceptibly and it
shakes me.

            She woke us. I shut our door to contain
her cries (we have others in the next room),
to wipe the vomit, invisible and tangy, from
her lips. She is hungry from emptying milky stomach
contents across her pack-and-
play, stunned by the violence of it
violent, and so are your insides, little
one...
      there.
I will hold your head in my hand.

We take shifts, and the first is mine. My wife will feed her soon.

In the night I press her cries skin-to-skin, and
she roots, snuffling for a full breast. Some nights I pray
to not feel empty in the face of hunger, or futile
to grant my lover sleep.
                       We are born and frantic to fill
our bellies, frantic to fill our insides with
rest but it doesn't settle in
the early days. Until she takes solid food
milk will never be enough.

My lover wakes after the change, at the full wet thud
of the diaper in the bin, and pivots wearily sideways
as a priest to a worshipper, crouched to present the cup.
"The body of your Mother, opened for you."

Her preparatory cough is
stifled, latched, and she cradles
her head in her fists, taking, taking, taking. I will
lodge myself (human, husband, pillow), prop
up the warmth to ease the strain
as she uncoils
in our arms.

We sleep until we wake again
the fragile ritual repeats, little
one...

       there.
her heart in the palm of my hand.

ii. safe no more

I was walking to the train station
reading of an active shooter lockdown drill.
The teacher's youngest student was terrified
by the fake shooter pounding at the door
and clung to her, as skin to a bone,
the only supporting structure in an
institution designed for safety and growth,
(safe no more, walls notwithstanding)
where striking real fear into children
is a necessary part of the curriculum.

It was his birthday.
But he must know how to hide, should
the day we all dread come knocking
at the door, armed and angry.

On every western track of Union Station
the trains stand, running, delayed
because someone walked onto the track
one stop from mine and ended it.
The authorities can't release
us until they clear the area.
The mind is vivid, too vivid,
like imagining my child held in
arms other than mine, her heart
pounding in her chest against the fear.

"We are cleared to depart."
The train slips forward slow,
in reverence
at the lives we've lost.

When we pass the place
the unnamed one stopped
there's a white tarp with dark marks on it
and some red bags lit by flashing blues,
and officers search the tracks with tiny lights for
something.
I'm late to hold my children
because one of us
broke.

I pass by
hundreds of people a day on my way to work.
I travel with
hundreds of normal people a day with "guns" on their lips and
shoulders bearing things you just don't talk about.
I see
hundreds of children holding red bags and clinging
to supporting structures and shining tiny lights to find something.

I think
we missed it.
I try not to think
at all.

I go home and hold my children.

iii. birdless

It was small and fast and had no
nest and no parents we could see. My children
were there and of course, we caught it.
We mashed up cat food and fed it through a straw.
My oldest daughter named it, so it was ours,
if only for a day. They held it like it would fly away
if they let it go, and it chirped
because it knew it couldn't.

Tomorrow they get up early
to see it and it's dying, I can see that
but they think it's only sleeping. Google says
that mobile baby birds are meant to bounce around,
getting help from parents only when needed,
so that they learn to feed themselves.
We fed it, so it's dying.

I tell them we have to let it go,
and my daughter cries when I carry it out
on the broad blade of the shovel to the
back acre and leave it on a pile of leaves.
I tell her not to follow me, but she does.
I stand there willing it to hop away, but it won't.

My heart is in my hand as we walk back birdless,
and I give it to her to hold so that she knows
I understand and won't ever understand.
We cry as one at the loss and she grows a little more
in the way I wish she wouldn't.

If I could change one thing in the
world we live in, it might be this:
not that birds die, or that my child knows it now,
for if I blinded her to each loss
she might never love birds at all;
but that it was by our hands,
holding helpful, feckless hearts.

leech

take it.
take hold of it.

take it like a gator
pinning prey, a leech
sucking life-blood, a dog
locking its jaws, a lifer
eating his last meal, a lush
draining the dregs, a gambler
rolling the dice, a pyro
lighting a match, a newborn
pinching a finger, a dying thief,
a weeping mother, the maw
of an open grave, take it:

this bread and this wine,
with the desperation
of the once-damned,

and live.

call and response

I believe in the power of the broken
to attract,
like blooms, precarious
on the stem. They cast
nectar-sweet lines to passing bees,
fluted stanzas on a summer's day.

Pass me by
if you will,
but it will do your heart good
to shelter here
and sip
the bitter with the sweet.

rainplay

The pit-pat of rain
and little feet,
the splash of a puddle then,
like liquid laughter, and
the storm is just another
plaything
to tiny toes.

quiet

You are not quiet, my love.
You shout like an Indiana
evening, a cacophony carried
close to my chest. You yearn
like pre-dawn fog to dissolve
in new heat. You cry out for more,
noon upon my brow, beating
me backward with your thirst.

You are not quiet, my love,
like the warning before a dusk
of thunder and downpours. You
are not the sun-bleached thicket
when I get too close, when every
creature holds its breath.
You are not midnight.

My heart, you beat within me,
beyond the light, a creature
crashing through in fright at being
found, and I cannot catch
a glimpse of you, for you are
audible and absent to the
eye, essential to the soul,
spurious. You are air, but
you are not
quiet.

Riddle me this, my love,
When will you be still?
For then, over naked fields
after the harvest
of all things,
I may see you as you are.

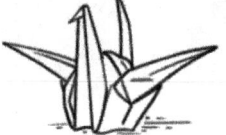

AUTUMN

chicago in season

iv.

This morning I saw
the moon, a sliver eclipsed
beside a single star.

--

The plastic bag ghost
strained for freedom, ankle snagged
by brittle branches.

--

They belly up to
the truck hood and sip coffee
to slow the day down.

--

Chicago's a beater.
She thrums and glistens, waits for
dawn to rev to life.

--

He does magic tricks
for the sake of a smile and
a couple bucks. Watch.

familiars

The day arrived
when the darkness crept in
like a lame animal
and wrapped itself
round my feet in repose.
It sighed, and I sighed,
and I put out
a plate of leftovers
and let it stay the night.

through fathoms

That evening in the leaf pile
my daughter told me that the sky was the sea,
and the trees many-tentacled.

We shrieked, delighted
at their awful suckered limbs,
and hid beneath the pilings of the nearest weathered pier.
The current took them past us,
and she giggled in the reef.

Perhaps the moon shone down
from higher skies, through oceans clear as air,
or maybe it was phosphorus undulating through the waves.
Whatever it was that lit the deep,
we paddled on through auburn piles
and swam among the seaweed in our path.

And as we lay looking up
through fathoms
speckled with brown and yellow schools of falling fish,
the deep, deep sky reflected back the smile
and we felt free
in the peaceful rush of the tide.

We saw and understood something
of life and its mercies,
leagues below the sky.

blanks

Patches are missing,
but I catch something blurry in the space.
I don't even know that I miss it until I dig up past days.
It moved so fast,
and presence isn't a strength of mine, so it's possible
that I didn't impress each length of time,
as wildflower or fallen leaf,
between the pages of my mind.

The mild power of most memories
isn't freeze-framed like family photos,
or captured on VHS, in stunning granularity.
When I watch the ones I own, they're trite,
as if I wrote down the wrong things in my journal,
the memory without the meaning.

But there must be meaning to those blanks,
not just noise without impact,
because sometimes they flicker and appear, intact,
with the wild power of familiarity:
A face, a smell, the pace of a yellow atmosphere at a certain time of day.
Most of my fears
cascade in curtains of rhymes between me, myself, and I,
but the ones that ambush me
part the sea, my hell, and the sky.

It could be, like existence and wonders unexplored,
that this thunder by the door, these bullets to the brain,
are kept in safekeeping to the fullness of the day
that I am most in need (most days, it seems).
Most days I could use a dream, or two or three.

So you and me? Let's leave them lie, let them sleep.
Someday every fragment will have risen from the deep
and we,
memory-dancers all, just maybe we won't care.
since the ephemeral answer seems
to be in getting there.

US-20 in october

The wind is witty today,
peeling back the clouds
like banana peels and leaving
them lying around yellow for someone
to slip on, and I laugh at the thought of it.

Smell that smoke! We are
a trundling caravan of modern covered wagons,
lyrical spokes, outriders, a jeep, a hearse,
a family van, a sports car, a truck wielding
a home — yes, the smoke of a million
internal combustions. Everyone is burning
broad banks of leaves, collecting ashes
for when we all fall down, and the smoke follows us
like a stray dog, and we weep when we see
its ribs and promise to feed it when we return.

The earth roasts itself to a tawny golden crisp
and all things bend lower, further, deeper
until they crack like the longest beam,
plunging sparks down into extinguished rest.
The ash will settle, cooling from white to red
to black to white, and there we will be,
a dense cloud
of witnesses traipsing to the west.

bleeding in, bleeding out

All the time I knew
you carried weight upon your back
in every tremor when you spoke,
in every "I could never..." disbelief;
as if the sin that you held close
was when you reached out to receive.

All the ways I knew
you bought such shame for taking time
in every conversation held,
how all the grasping proved the need
within a hungry heart undone,
that, reaching out, still could not feed.

Now the platitudes weigh heavy
like our waiting in the night
beneath the cold fluorescent lights.
Forgive me, sister —
all the time I knew
you, I never knew this.

As bleeding weeps, so bleeding speaks.
I'll take your wrist and wish it true:
that you would let me
bleed with you.

suspension lament

I'm angry
at the pundits at the top that crush
the people down below them, at the
bent backs breaking beneath boots shod with blood —
when leading equals leaving,
bleeding "them" for what you love
(green paper, power trails).
We're seething here as justice fails.

See the first cause running deep,
steeped in and reaping sin, all of us
echoing status changes
round padded mirrored rooms
riddled with fad-filled mirrored tombs...
I'm being myself,
I'm seeing myself
and I'm broken. I'm broken.

I'm livid at You, Lord,
Who let's us free to run our games —
to stun, to lame, to blame,
to see our efforts falling short.
Tether me fast against the blast of my lungs,
sin speaking from within, sleek sonnets of soot and ash.
I'm greedy, I'm rash
for the justice I don't see you wielding.
Can't you remake your made-people yielding?

I am seeing
in Your Word: wrath withheld

                      (Lord, have mercy)

and justice untouched by the All-Power,
all of us, flowers, much in need,
born of seeds scattered.

                      (Christ, have mercy)

We matter.
We all do,
we all of us, matter to You,
and that's why the weight of justice waits
— by suspension: redemption
by lack: grace —

                      (Spirit, have mercy)

In You we live livid and grieve
and salve our seeing,
and let justice fail a little while, long,
and lift the dying, failing, fleeing,
until we cease to hum along
and thrum in holy, living Song.

ode to autumn

May autumn tinge me inward,
dip me in its auburn waves
under heavens of molten brass,
and hang me upside down
to wither and dry in the shivering sun.
For then, I'll make good eating when winter
shuffles the color aside.

All the earth is bloodied and bruised,
and the purple smell of the over-ripe
hangs by a thread,
ready to tumble to rot,
to fall from living to dead.
The bushes are burning;
who could know
that hell on earth is holy, as incense in the tomb?
The impulse to remove my shoes
rises to bloodlust in my veins.

I would fall prostrate in the ashes,
in delight at such a death
that bears abundance on its back.

but now I see

All these years alone
on the inside with a smile
smeared, my words dripping
down the back of my throat --
the things I would never speak
out loud:

I am in the arms of my mother,
her sweater leaving lines across my face.
I stack the faux-pearls along her necklace.
Now I am hiding
behind the pew,
stacking hymnals. They dance
in circles around the room and I
hope they can't see me hiding,
or make me dance.

I'm sick to my stomach
but I'm one of them regardless.
I toe the line, I kick against the goads,
I am blind
but now
                I see, I am dead
but now
                I am alive
but now
I am the arms of someone
finding "faith, hope, love" scribbled
on a torn bulletin, with a crude
sketch of a monster
scrunched up where the hymnals should be
stacked — it won't fit —

but now
                I see
it doesn't need to.

bon-fire

Before it got too dark to see
we gathered
fallen leaves
and snap-dry sticks

and tepeed them there
in the pit.

My father crumpled up
yesterday's newspaper,
my brother struck the match.

With our backs to the night,
we gathered
together, half of each
lit like the underside of a leaf.
We stayed
until the flames
licked the bones
down to coals,

and spoke our stories
over the ash.

crowns

Late in the year, the autumn
is lauding the tall ones, lined
up trunk to trunk, and I jostle one
and ask the question. "Why,
it's all about perception," he winks
and pats my head.
"When you're older
you'll understand."

So I wait and watch
the days go by, and each figure
is capped with gold,
is seen and loved
and stands up taller than the rest
for but a little while.

For once the year is out
they droop, clutching
for windfalls. I asked one once,
as it raked its limbs through frost,
what it was
it looked for. It snapped

at me, "my dignity!"
But that was long gone,
Like the crowded roar of fall.
He gave way then,
an old man
of an old way.

I must have been older then,
for I looked to my forehead
and saw only grey, and knew
the crowns we gather now
will one day fall away.

perhaps the sea

Foaming and violent as the wave,
we echo of beatings taken
on shores unknown or known too well.
The sea is as young as it is sage,
as seasoned in relief as spite,
splitting sand and salt asunder
in its desperate grasp for land.
Within our breasts beat
echoes of a land taken, grain by grain —
we know not where or when.
Leagues and knots rattle
and roll on by beneath us,
scraping our hulls, lulling us,
pulling parabola ripples back
and forth and back, and finally forth.
We are parabolic too.

The sea and sky, each inside the other,
entwine and boil as aquamarine,
fallible, flawed and two things at once: one new thing.
The oldest things — perhaps
the deepest things — fail us
at the moment of resurgence,
for they shift beneath our feet and
we are walking on air with our heads in the ocean.
The upside will be down,
on all sides sea as far as the eye,
on every side beings of import and export believe.

We are waves and sand and sea and sky,
grey and blue and green and black,
and one day there will no more of us,
(by virtue or valor, the earth will be full of us),
and the sky will consume the sea and send it
back and forth on the wind
as judgment and serene volition.

wanton

I cannot shake you. You cling like my lips to my guilt,
like my ears to my lies, like my back to my shame, you cling
and I cannot shake you. They say I am the one who held you
but wrestling doesn't work that way. I would take hold of the bruise:
a symbol of the time you stopped me, an ode to the song you sang me,
a scar to the blood beneath. I am limping with the longing to be near you —
as the bread is broken and the blood spilt
and I sit in a distant pew dripping wine on the stone I call home,
a house for he who lives here still, for the wanting will not cease.

I eat, and I drink, and I am merry. But the wine is red and
the blood from the blow is on my lips — a rarity, precious,
carmine, rubies. A wanton need it is, this urgency to leap
to the struggle, to pin you down, to lay you out, to rest
in your arms. In the tension of pulling away there is solace.
"And also with you," you whisper as you dislocate my limbs —
as the bread is broken and the blood spilt,
and I sit in the distant pew dripping wine on the stone I call home,
a house for me, who lives here still, for I cannot cease to want you.

and there will come a time

I used to believe that there would come a time
when I believed enough, or
worked enough,
or loved the good things long enough,
or hated the bad things hard enough,
that I would be
obedient, and holy, and righteous,
that I would love
rightly, and live as such.

But now I believe that
there will come a time, and it will come
over and over until I believe,
like each season after the last,
or the dawn after the night
or the rainbow tilting in the sky after the judgment of the rain,
that God will speak
again of His unrelenting love for me,
He will call me His child,
Yes —
He will name me His child again,
and I will hear it and believe.

That time is now, and soon, and forever,
a repeating sound of truth and joy
over the cacophony of shame in my ear
that attempts to silence His love.

He is gentle,
and He repeats Himself a lot,
and that's why I love Him so.

burn on steady

Burn on steady, child,
find the fire in your veins
and stoke it, tend it 'til
it billows into flames,
until the roaring is your name.

Flow in currents, child,
find the river running wide
and rend it, split it 'til
it rises on each side
until the contour is your bride.

Soar on mistrals, child,
find the gale in your wings
and ride it, hover 'til
it births a world of kings,
until the sparrow in you sings.

Grow in deeper, child,
find the soil in your soul
and mine it, tunnel 'til
it yields a crop of coal
until the furnace makes you whole.

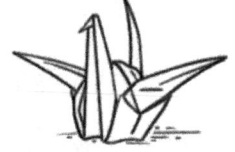

From Chris...

To the merry poets of the Poetry Pub: Thank you for keeping me laughing and writing poetry, and for planting the seed of this book last November.

To Chris Yokel, Jen Yokel, Rachel Donahue, and Shigé Clark: Thank you for your invaluable critique and encouragement, and for showing me how fun making a poetry book could be.

To Josie: For taking a tiny germ of an idea and making an entire mythos out of it. This collaboration has been on the books for a long time, and I'm thrilled that we finally did it!

To my children: Thanks for making it difficult for me to find time to write poetry, and for inspiring almost all of it by teaching me how to truly see the world.

To Linnea: You told me to not compromise on my vision, you spurred me on through the process, and you made the space for me to create. Thanks for being my strength and spine through all of this. You're incredible.

To my Heavenly Father: Thanks for giving me words, and a heart to receive them.

From Josie...

To my Snowball: You are the best cat ever.

To Chris: Your work is beautiful, and your friendship lifegiving.

To my David: My gratitude is unspeakable.

To my God: Everything.

the giving of thanks

To all of the following incredible people, who believed in this book and made it a reality with their support: Thank you. You have made our year! We hope that this book is as much of an encouragement to you as you have been to us.

Edward Arnold
John and Janna Barber
Adrian and Kristin Breems
Elizabeth Dailing
Lianna Davis
Rachel Donahue
Daniel Emme
Dustin Franks
Amelia Friedline
Mom and Dad Greene
Tina Gregg
Karley Hepworth
Jesse Hübner
Allison Keeport
Sarah Lang
Joshua Lee
Thomas Leonard
Beth Mason

Hannah Mitchell
Kyle Newberry
Daniel and Kelsey Park
Melany Patrascu
Nate and Anna Petersheim
Lynn Pottenger
Sharon Robbert
Kimberly Schmurr
Faith Snowden
Robert Spangler
Caleb Tolleson
Jack Underwood
Barbara Videtich
Mom and Dad Wheeler
Justin Wilhelmsen
Julianne Wonser
Chris Yokel

Chris Wheeler is a writer and poet based out of Middlebury, IN. His nonfiction, liturgies, and poetry have been published in Barren, Fathom, Kingdoms in the Wild, Reformed Worship, Foundling House, and The Rabbit Room, among others. He lives with his wife and five children in his childhood home.

Read more from him at chriswheelerwrites.com, or follow along on Instagram @chriswheelerwrites or @solacepoems.

Josie Koznarek is a fine artist based in Chicago, IL. Working primarily in ink paintings, Josie identifies the primal thread tying the individual person to all of nature, finding release and freedom in grounding one's self to the connectedness of the world.

You can see and purchase her work at jkoznarek.com, and keep up to date with her current projects on Instagram @jkoznarek.

www.ingramcontent.com/pod-product-compliance
Lightning Source LLC
Chambersburg PA
CBHW071356160426
42811CB00112B/2312/J